In Lisa Dordal's stunning second collection *Water Lessons*, she pivots from the political to the personal, from despair to unapologetic delight, revealing that one cannot exist without the other. In the title poem "Water Lessons" she writes, "In Leningrad, I was told not to drink / the water. It could cause illness; / in rare cases, death" ending the poem, "I drank the water": both a confession and reclamation of self, as if to create an inventory of what might cause harm, and then walk us directly into the damage. In this way, Dordal tends to the messy and uncertain realms of the heart, capturing what it is to long for what we know will hurt us, and how we are nourished by that longing: "Remember *mother* // contains not just the sea / but the darkness of the sea. // And there is no such thing / as a half-life for grief." I read *Water Lessons* the way I would look through an old family photo album; the ache of nostalgia and regret in one hand, joy and forgiveness in the other. Lisa Dordal is a poet of exquisite craft and grace, unafraid to face what haunts her, knowing that this is where the treasure lies. This book is the treasure.

—Kendra DeColo, author of *I Am Not Trying to Hide My Hungers from the World*

water lessons

Poems

Lisa Dordal

www.blacklawrence.com

Executive Editor: Diane Goettel
Cover Design: Zoe Norvell
Book Design: Amy Freels
Cover Art: "The Bright Day #580", oil on panel, 48" x 48", 2017 by Louise LeBourgeois

Copyright © Lisa Dordal 2022
ISBN: 978-1-62557-031-4

Published 2022 by Black Lawrence Press.
Printed in the United States.

For my mother, who always wanted to write,
for my father, whom I love more than words can say,
and for Laurie (again)

Contents

I

Welcome

Flipping the remote, I keep landing
on the hotel's Welcome Channel.

Hello, a woman says. White woman,
pretty smile. *May I have a minute of your time?*

Be as alert as you are at home, she says.
Pretty woman, concerned for my safety.

She keeps walking towards me—there,
behind everything else. Like fear behind the eyes.

I keep flipping, taking in the news of the week.
People are protesting in the streets:

This Pussy Fights Back. No Ban, No Wall.
Never invite strangers into your room.

Pretty smile, pretty woman. As pretty
as my mother was when she was alive.

Pretty as she was in my dream. *Be alert,*
the woman says. *As alert as you are at home.*

I never knew, on Tuesdays, what she'd look like—
my mother, who drove to the Del Mar College

of Hair Design to get dolled up cheap
by a stranger. Sometimes large, loopy curls.

Other times, tight and small—tucked in
like something sleeping. *Use the viewport,*

the woman says, *if someone knocks on your door.*
Hepburn-chestnut one week to a sassy blonde

the next. In the dream, she is reading
from my book. She looks happy.

Keep the doors and windows locked,
the woman says. In five pages,

my mother will be dead. First, the bottles
hidden in bookcases throughout

the house. Then, the heart wing. *Locked,*
the woman says, *at all times.* My mother

glances up. She is reading in the voice she used
for *Sounder* and *The Chronicles of Narnia.*

She reads as if the woman she is
will not die; as if the woman who dies

will not be her. As if she is not even *there.*
Like when she learned about my attempts—

aspirin, then the knife, my hand like Abraham's
over Isaac. *Nice story,* my mother said.

We had learned to slip out of ourselves.
To squeeze our consciousness through a hole

the size of a dime. We were small inside
our bodies. My body is sin, she told me once.

Be alert, the woman says. *As alert
as you are at home. Nice story,* she said.

Water Lessons

My mother loved the beach at 57th Street
where she'd stand at the water's edge,
her head bent to a magazine.
I never saw her swim.

*

Sometimes I still hear her
walking the halls of our house—
the sound of ice clinking
against the inside of her glass.
The sound of her breathing
on the other side of the door.

*

Alcohol is absorbed into the body
through the bloodstream.
Alcohol affects every part of the body.
Liver, stomach, eyes, brain.

Heart.

*

Inside the Titanic,
there is a glass of water
still sitting on a bureau—
the strange physics
that allowed drowning,
not breaking.

*

Sometimes I still hear her
climbing the stairs of our house.
The sound of ice against glass.

*

As a child, I feared falling
into the soft, leaky ice
that barely covered the fields
where we skated.

*

In Leningrad, I was told not to drink
the water. It could cause illness;
in rare cases, death.

*

Salmon can smell the distant waters
of their birth, towards which they swim
when they are ready to spawn.

*

In Leningrad, I drank the water.

Backstory

When owls hunt at night
they see our version of day

shadowed by clouds. Concurrence
of dark and light, like the gods

I memorized as a child—
Father, Son, and Holy Ghost.

How I learned the Creed
by heart, as if love must be

drilled into us. *Father Almighty,*
Maker of all things seen

and unseen. I could recite
any number of statistics—

God of God, Light of Light—
one in three women

assaulted. Growing up,
I could press my ear

to any wall in our house,
and hear the murmuring

of male voices, like a swarm
of bees. *Begotten, not made,*

being of one substance
with the Father.

Ars Poetica

My mother is saying something I still can't hear.

And I want to believe there is a door.

Sometimes I dream I am being led through darkness.

And I wouldn't call her death "natural."

So many rooms were closed off before we knew they were there.

And I was the one no one believed.

And my father still insists her liver was fine.

It was her heart, he says, *just her heart.*

Underpinnings

The house presses
into the girl
and the girl becomes
the house and the house
becomes the girl.

The girl accepts the force
of her father's
voice; his words
against her skin.

The house presses
into her. And the girl becomes
small and quiet
like a statue pulled from an old grave—
wide staring eyes, a mouth
that could be chanting
or screaming.

Grief

There will be days when the word mother
will burst out of you

like the black smoke of a squid, a fire
deep inside water. Anyone can become

animal or a flicker of light.
Remember infinity

means unfinished,
and time doesn't move

at the same speed for everyone.
Remember *mother*

contains not just the sea
but the darkness of the sea.

And there is no such thing
as a half-life for grief.

Even oceans contain waterfalls
and your mother is inside

everything that you write—
sometimes as melody,

sometimes as mountain
or bone. Every time

you hear the word, you become
something else.

Of One Substance

Even the field
where the girl runs

is filled with the sound
of bees, low hum

darkening the sky.
This murmuring

that enters her, thinks itself
divine. To survive

she becomes like the body
of any small thing—

a worm in black dirt,
a wing pressing

into mud.

Interview

Tell me about yourself.

My mother is dead.
I write poems about her.
Sometimes it feels like she is alive.
It's a game we play.
I play. She watches.
Always, she is watching.

What was she like?

She was beautiful.

What else?

She was my mother.

And?

She sang to us.
She took us shoe shopping at Gately's on 53rd.
She drove a blue Karmann Ghia.
She had her hair done every Tuesday.
She helped people. Out there,
in the world, she helped people.

And?

At night, she disappeared.
She was in the house,
she was not in the house.
She looked past everything that was in front of her.

What was she looking for?

I don't know.

Did it scare you, this looking?

It scared me. It didn't scare me.

Which answer is true?

Yes, it scared me.

Meditations on My Mother's Death

When my father sends me the clear plastic bottle
that used to contain forty-two pink and grey capsules—

the Darvon 65 my mother took for pain
in the days following my birth—

I keep it. The words: *Six times daily* and *May be habit-forming*
typed onto the once-white label.

The task of sorting possessions, endless and peculiar—
everyone offering advice about how to proceed.

Get rid of her clothes first.
Don't sell the house for a year.

*

Millions of unseen organisms die every second—
silent, bloodless—still

I am surprised by it. A chickadee's skull
is thin & white. Energy,

I am told, is never gained or lost.

*

In the kitchen there was a boy—
a small metal boy with a small metal penis—

proud and erect atop a pedestal. As my father
pushed a flat black button, out came whiskey into a glass.

Could never be a girl. The unseemly squat.
Or standing there, wet whiskey on her thighs.

*

Photographs make the dead living—
my mother raising a glass on Christmas Eve,

her mouth, even now, saying *Prosit*—
and the living, dead.

*

My grandfather—mother's side—
couldn't make it back home from our house

without stopping. *Always the same spot,*
my cousin told me. He'd stop the car,

walk to the edge of the lot and piss
into the mess of scraggly bushes.

*

In a recent photo, taken by a stranger
only for the moon behind it, the house appears—

larger, with an added floor. An iron gate
surrounds the property. The window shades

are pulled to the sills. Energy is never gained or lost.
I tell myself to be happy. I tell myself

the house has been sold.   17

My Mother, Arriving

My mother walks backwards in an old family movie.
The same scene over and over. Leaving,

then arriving. She's wearing cat-eye sunglasses,
a navy blue pantsuit, and a pewter peace necklace.

The only sound is the hum of the projector.
She smiles, waves *hello*. My father

is invisible behind the lens. The week she died,
we cleaned the house for something to do,

turned lights on and off in rooms we didn't know we were in.

Each stroke, Cezanne said, *must contain the air,*
the light, the object. My mother,

walking towards our house; my mother,
waving to my father. My father, invisible behind the lens.

*

In a movie about a failed art heist, a thief
walks slowly up the main staircase in a library.

Students are studying for exams, violins play
in the background. And a voice says:

Are you okay? The thief continues up the stairs.
The music gets louder. *Is there a doctor in the house?*

Someone from the front row stands up, walks
to the middle of the theater where a man is sitting—

head back, mouth open. *Sir?* a voice says.
The movie freezes. *Are you okay?*

*

Now, when my father says: *Your mother and I,*
he gestures towards his new wife.

He doesn't allow her to mention her late husband.
She tells me stories when we're alone—

as much as she can before my father enters the room.
They were married forty years.

Does he ever mention her? I ask.
Never, she says. Both of us, equally sad.

My father is invisible behind the lens.
The man in the theater was fine. My mother

waves *hello.* I keep stumbling out of her,
holding my hands up to the light.

My mother, arriving. My mother, leaving.
My mother, not going away.

II

Postcards from the 70s

Hyde Park, Chicago

I.

When the man from three houses down asks
if he can take my picture, I say sure.

He's a renter—lives alone on the top floor
of a neighbor's house—wants me to meet him there.

I see him every morning when I walk the dog.
I talk about poems because he's a poet too.

I talk about school, my after-school job.
I tell him I used to take piano, but never practiced.

He takes a draw from his pipe, watches me
through the smoke. Saturday, he says.

Don't wear a turtleneck, he says.

2.

On the west side of Regenstein Library,
there's a large bronze statue in the shape of a human head—
the face of the first self-sustaining
nuclear chain reaction hardened into steel.
Smooth and round, with tunnels
our small bodies can worm through.

3.

My mother wears dresses to fundraisers and parties and the opera.
My father wears a suit or a black tux.

On a Friday afternoon I'm watching TV at Sarah's house
(best friend, sophomore year)

and Sarah's mother appears suddenly in the doorframe of the family room—
like the angel appearing suddenly to Mary—

to ask: *Long or short?* I'm supposed to know
she's talking about the length of my mother's dress.

And, of course, I know.

4.

My mother tells me when I grow up, I will be as well-off as Wendy's
    family is now.
My mother tells me every generation is wealthier than the one before.
My mother tells me we are climbing a ladder.
My mother tells me we are going higher and higher.

5.

I eat lunch every day with two white guys—
popular, smart, college-bound. I'm fourteen,

they're sixteen. I hear their cheerfulness
every time they greet the hall guard—

an older black woman—stationed
outside the cafeteria. I see them smiling

as they walk by calling out to her,
saying softly to me, *watch this*. I see

her feigned look of politeness when they
call her the name they have given her,

when they say *Good afternoon*, smiling
and waving. *Good afternoon, Mrs. Rhesus.*

I can't un-hear my laughter.

6.

The sound of Rockefeller Chapel's carillon every Saturday at noon.

The sound of seventy-two bells and a hundred tons of bronze.

The sound of barely heard things—

the way a bird says *drink your tea* or *teacher, teacher, teacher*—

things like *Father, Son, Sky.*

And *Not you, not you, not you.*

7.

After my first week filing charts at the hospital, Jeanette—a full-timer—
asks whether I go to Lab (the private school) or Kenwood (public).

We're in a crowded corridor, heading towards the Ellis Avenue exit.
Outside, she'll go right (towards 60th) and I'll go left.

Kenwood, I say, which I can tell is the right answer.
Soon we're chatting on the phone in the evenings.

When her daughter answers, I hear *It's that white girl* in the background.
When Jeanette calls, my mother says—as if to be polite—*I think it might
    be Jeanette.*

Sometimes we go to Looey's on Cottage Grove for hot dogs and fries.
We both know, without saying it, that she's my bodyguard.

Whenever my mother and I drive past Looey's on the way
to someplace else, I think: *I've been there*. As if that was something.

I Remember

I remember *Sail Away*, *Freak Out*, and *Shining Star*.
I remember the burn of vodka on the back of my throat,
the nuclear war that never happened and the winter that never followed.

I remember my mother looking right through me
and thunderstorms just being thunderstorms.

I remember my boyfriend letting me drive his yellow station wagon in the
    parking lot
behind the Museum of Science and Industry.

I remember being beautiful, then ugly. And the twins
who had a special dance for every song.

I remember my father picking me up at the house of someone I didn't
    know—
the living room crowded with drunk, slow-dancing teenagers
and my father looking like he didn't know how to reach me.

I remember Brooke Shields making a movie in our neighborhood
and all the boys falling for her.

I remember a black guy from gym class calling me Mary half a dozen times.
I remember telling him *I'm not Mary* and him saying:
You white people all look alike. I remember wanting to hug him.

I remember riding up and down 53rd Street in the backseat of someone's
    convertible,
Take It on the Run blasting from the speakers, over and over.

I remember Gwendolyn Brooks calling to say she liked my poem.
I remember wearing a black turtleneck to school the next day and the next.

I remember my father telling me my mother didn't really have to work
and I might not either and something inside me getting smaller and
    smaller.

I remember asking a friend what she thought happens when we die—
we were playing cards on her porch and it smelled like rain.

I remember someone's older sister stopped eating
and feeling like it was all a bad dream.

I remember being happy when it snowed.
I remember looking up into the sky and watching the world come down
one piece at a time.

III

My Mother Is a Peaceful Ghost

In my dreams my mother keeps walking out of the kitchen singing
You are my sunshine, my only sunshine.

She never sings past the first verse.

Last night, I dreamed I was back at the house—
every light on when I arrived. My mother, forgetting

she was dead, smiled, said she was fine, everything
was fine. At family gatherings—weddings, baptisms—

my mother would look around, sort of stunned,
and say: *There're so many of you!* As if

we'd arrived from some place other than her
own body, a country foreign to her. My mother

is no longer flesh or breath. She's not a *thing*
anymore. Is she with God?

Some days I believe, some days I don't.
Centuries ago, in a church in Europe,

someone carved *God Help Us* into a pew.
Plague years. Sometimes my god is so big,

I wonder what's the use. Divinity
diluted into nothingness. My mother

tried to stop drinking. *I stopped*, she told me once.
Like you'd stop a dryer or a washing machine.

We were standing in the Blackwater Falls gift shop
looking at coffee mugs printed with maps.

West Virginia on one side, waterfalls on the other.
One mug had a gold star to mark the visitor center.

You Are Here, on a travel mug. Here and
not here. How do you name what isn't here?

She tried to stop. And didn't.

Housekeeper

Memory is a tough place. You were there.
—Claudia Rankine

Her last name started with R.
Robertson or Richardson. First name, Willa.

Twice a week she vacuumed,
dusted tabletops, dressers,

the piano we rarely used; fixed lunch for us.
And dinner on Monday nights

when my mother worked late—
meatloaf topped with bacon,

or chicken peppered in a pan of white rice.
She took the Jeffery Express up Stony Island to 57th

from several neighborhoods south—
the same bus I took as a teenager

to go north to Marshall Fields
where women in high heels walked the aisles

armed with tester bottles of perfume—
Charlie, Obsession, Chanel #5.

Did I ever know her last name?
We went to public schools, marched

in Grant Park (for peace, I think). My father
put stickers in the windows of businesses

that promised not to discriminate.
We were good people. The good kind of white.

But how good could any of us be?
I read, even loved, Pippi Longstocking,

ate Space Sticks and Captain Crunch,
watched *The Brady Bunch* every Friday night.

Everything I did, inside something
I didn't know I was in. She came to our graduations,

later our weddings. I saw her.
I didn't see her. Was it Richardson?

Or Robertson? Our dog growled every Monday
when she arrived at our back door,

and, again, on Friday. She was alone with him
for most of the day. Did he growl

each time she re-entered the kitchen
through the swinging door that separated

the butler's pantry from the rest of the house?
We lived in a "nice" neighborhood.

How good could any of us be? The truth is:
memory is a hard, hard place. There is what happened.

And what didn't. Did our dog growl
each time Willa re-entered the kitchen?

I never asked.

Horses

My father is dying in Atlanta
in a house he doesn't own,

a city whose streets
he's never really learned.

Not like Kimbark, Kenwood, Dorchester—
streets in Chicago

he made us memorize,
made sure we always knew

where we were. He lives
with his second wife—

seventeen years in November.
They are ninety-one

though my father insists
he is ninety-four.

This isn't the gay nineties,
he quips, whenever age comes up.

And I laugh out of joy,
not obligation. Laughter,

my yoga teacher says,
is the holiest form of breathing.

And we breathe this way
until we don't.

He sleeps in a hospital bed
in the living room.

In front of him, above the mantle,
is a painting of eight,

maybe nine, horses running,
their bodies blurring

in an endless motion of browns and blacks.
He thinks the painting

is from Uncle Julius.
He is surrounded by artifacts

from his wife's first marriage,
which he makes his own,

placing them into narratives,
new and temporary.

The horses run and run,
never reaching their destination.

He thinks Uncle Julius is alive,
thinks he is coming over

for tea. *Nice*, I say.
And for a moment, it is.

Primer

You're a white girl, cute in the eyes,
reading your first chapter book.

Maybe it's summer and you're sitting
on the porch steps, painted red

every year by your mother. Maybe
the sky is blue and the elm trees

don't have Dutch Elm Disease.
Which means you haven't grieved yet

for a tree. Maybe this is the day
your father will set up the swimming pool,

with its thick plastic floor and round
corrugated wall. Maybe soon

you'll feel the pieces of dark mulch
poking up from beneath the plastic.

Maybe you loved the bumpiness
of the pool floor because you knew

how to float above it. It wasn't a big pool
but you were small. Your body fit

everywhere. Under porches when you played
Twelve O'clock the Witch Comes Out.

Or inside the house (cupboards,
sideboards). Maybe this is the day

you're reading Pippi Longstocking,
the year you loved Pippi best.

Her house by the sea, her horse,
her strength. The ease with which

she travelled the world. Maybe
you're already thinking about Halloween,

painting your face with freckles,
putting hangers in your hair

to make your braids stick out.
Maybe you didn't think anything

about the "barbarians"
in the Congo, didn't understand

the part about Pippi's father
being King of the Negroes.

Maybe you saw the picture of Pippi
with her face painted black,

and turned the page the way
you turned any page. White girl

inside the white imagination.
The horse, the tiny house,

the beautiful ocean. Before you knew
an ocean could be anything

but beautiful.

Love Poem

I love how the words
My Mother and I

are like a door, slightly open,
the darkness itself

peeking out.
I love the hunger

of a baby bird
showing its red infinity

to the world. I love
three kinds of consciousness—

flesh, ghost, divine.
I love the blue vein

beneath the skin
of my right wrist—

how it forgave me
immediately.

Sheltering in Place

A friend reminded me recently of joy—
my joy. My laugh, infectious, she said. She's remembering

the games we played in seventh grade.
Dialing random numbers from the phone book—

Tell me a story, we'd say to whoever answered. I need stories
to survive. The daughter I don't have making angels

in a foot of new snow. Or sometimes *angles*
because the confusion delights her—lying down

once, then again, stretched out against her own
otherness. My niece, at three, is afraid of angels.

Please, Mommy, not the angels, she says
whenever her mother sings *Angels watching over me,*

my Lord. She doesn't like the idea of being watched
by something she can't see. There's a kind of spider

that sees as well as a cat. We saw one—my wife and I—
pacing on the railing of our front porch. It stared at us,

we stared back. Its body, the shape of a tiny gorilla.
Darwin said the eye gave him a cold shudder. I want a story

that ends in joy. I want to enter a house in which every window is open—
it's just beginning to rain and there's my mother

hurrying to shut each one. Moving through the house
with the urgency of a bird, trapped inside. One pane,

then another. Only, she isn't trying to leave.
She wants to stay.

Love Poem for My Father

In the cartoon, three angels are blindfolded like kids
at a birthday party, beating an earth-shaped piñata with sticks.

This one's full of nuts, the caption reads. Lately,
I imagine myself far from it—making the earth

so small, I can hold it in my hands. Everything smooth
and quiet. Like evidence from a previous extinction—

signature of dark rock different from what is above or below.
Enough to tell us something happened *here*, major,

irreversible. Silent now. My father's anger, waning
with his growing dementia. His face like a child's.

Occasional rage directed at the staff burdened with his care.
I hold his hand for a long time, taking a photo of just our hands,

quiet signature different from everything that came before.

A white girl describes her neighborhood, 1980

Like an island, the girl says. Eastern border,

Lake Michigan. Western, Cottage Grove.

She is sixteen. Flying west for vacation,

talking to a stranger, white like she is.

He laughs, the girl laughs. *Like an island.*

Northern border, 47th. Southern, 61st. Land

surrounded by water. Or something

resembling an island—isolated, detached,

surrounded in some way. Imaginary waters

with real waters inside. Cargo, suffocation,

the living shackled to the dead. White girl

carrying herself pleasantly. *Like an island.*

Everything below them, tiny.

Survival Guide for a Depressive

Draw a map, out of scale,
to the house where you grew up.
Draw snow, then rain.
Draw your mother
riding a horse in a state
she never mentioned.
Nebraska, perhaps.

*

Pretend you are the silhouette
of a woman you do not know.
Or a girl who smells faintly of lime.

*

Learn to hunt beetles and worms.
Declare yourself part shaman,
part musical bow.

*

Lie down beside the remains
of an old fire and pray
to the god you believe in. Pray
to the one that you don't.

*

Think of buried things:
teeth tucked into fissures;
craniums and seven small vases;
a sandal engraved with birds
and the words
Wear in good health.

　　　*

Raise your voice
to the Milky Way—
call it winter road
or backbone of night.

　　　*

Watch a flock of birds—
so many brains
all at once—in the sky.
Notice how the sky
begins at your feet.

　　　*

Draw three doors
on a sheet of paper. Look back
before you enter.

Broken Arm

Like you hold a baby, the nurse said. *Hold your arm*
like you hold a baby. And I held it that way.

My fingers fat with pain I couldn't feel
as I breathed *come back* onto my suddenly strange skin.

Like you hold a baby.

We had a son once. For a week calling him Ben.
A name the birth mother loved. And we loved

the way she said his name. Until she changed her mind
and the future became a house we weren't permitted to enter,

and the future became a great homesickness.
Which is how some traditions refer to the divine.

Which is to say everywhere and nowhere,
like salt dissolved in water. And now there is a boy

with a voice we can't hear, and a boy with a voice
we can't un-hear. A boy who might love darkness,

might love searching for constellations—
new ones that he can name. A boy

who makes dinosaurs from blue clay, each one
with three hearts. *You can't see them but they're there.*

Ben, the birth mother said. *Like you hold a baby*, the nurse said. Like a great homesickness

that might be god, or might be grief.

Dementia Bus

The glasses they give me
darken my vision, blur it

into shapes I can't immediately
recognize. I'm supposed to

set the table for breakfast,
write a check for the electric bill,

put on the brown jacket—
not the blue jacket—

and sort the shirts in the laundry basket—
long sleeved from short.

Every noun preceded by *the*
as if I live here, comfortably

surrounded by my life's
possessions. I'm wearing

oversized gloves to mimic arthritis,
spiky insoles for neuropathy.

I hear voices—simultaneously
loud and muffled—through headphones

that press heavily against my ears.
A few times, laughter

that stops too suddenly.
And a siren so loud I jump,

uttering *Get me out of here.*
To myself, I think. Except

there's a woman in the corner
watching me. She's taking notes.

She's too quiet. When I leave—
wearing the blue jacket,

not the brown jacket—
she gives me her notes

in which my failures are recorded
along with my words.

My father keeps merging
houses, first wife and second.

He knows me, he doesn't know me.
Sometimes he looks *into* my face

as if he's looking into a room,
darkened by night. When he was a boy,

he had to walk all the way
through his bedroom to reach

the room's only light switch.
I don't know if it's fear he feels now.

He thinks the house he lives in
has two piano rooms.

And when I visit, he sees birds
in the windows of my car.

I see leaves reflected and branches,
not birds. *Don't you see them,*

he asks. I'm not supposed to disagree.
Don't you? Sometimes he gives me clues

from the crossword puzzle.
Here's one for you, he says.

Part of LGBT, three letters,
starting with G. He's proud I came out.

Some days he thinks he's on a ship.
Some days he thinks he has patients to see,

meetings to attend. Some days
he sees birds in the windows

of my car. When I drive back home,
I take the birds with me.

My Mother Speaks to Me

She's in the hallway
of our old house,

looking towards me
but a little to one side,

and I'm not sure
which one of us is the ghost.

She doesn't blink
or smile. *Do you remember*

the alewives? she asks.
Thousands washed up

on the beach. Their
double-ringed eyes

staring and not staring.
A friend tells me I write

"mother poems,"
not poems about love

or death, but I don't know
the difference. Like seeing stars

reflected on a smooth surface
of water, and not knowing

if you're looking at the sea
or the sky. Voices, my mother says,

always return as echoes.
She tells me details

are infrequent; mostly
it's shapes, a vague sense

of something there,
not there—the hallway

suddenly empty,
a door creaking shut.

Daughter Poem

Sometimes I see her pressing her palms
against a windowpane in a house that is real

the way a house in a dream is real
until you start to describe it and all you can say is:

it was this house, only it wasn't. It's winter
and she likes to feel the cold entering her body.

Or it's summer and it's heat she's after.
She wasn't born, so she can't die.

Sometimes there is a window but no girl,
and I am the one walking towards it.

Sometimes I see her peering in—
forehead against the screen of our back door—

or running ahead of me on a path that is real
the way a path in a dream is real, saying:

this way, this way.

IV

The Last Time

The last time I saw my mother,
she was sitting in the front passenger seat

of my father's car. I looked down into her face
through the open window. She looked up at me

and smiled, said hello. Her right hand
resting on the door. She looked older

than her age, but beautiful.
And luminous. Something in her

already beginning to change. A seed,
buried in the ground, sensing the sun's

fuller light. She smiled, said hello.
Or maybe I was the seed, she the light.

I'm here, she said. And *here* was someplace else.

New Bird

There's a new bird at the feeder.
My stepmother notices its size. *Smaller,*

she says, *than a vireo or chickadee.*
My sister sees white on the wing.

I notice its beak, slender like a warbler's.
I open Peterson's *Field Guide to Birds*

and then, because it's November,
turn to Confusing Fall Warblers.

Four entire pages, as if confusion
were its own species. My father is with us

eating Cinnamon Crunch. He's a child
again, dementia changing his mind

daily. He's sweeter now, milder
than I've ever seen him. His own father

died when he was sixteen. Thanksgiving Day,
1943. *Sudden sickness of the heart,*

the paper said, above the outlook
for feed supplies and cattle costs.

The only time I've seen my father cry
was during *The Sound of Music,*

when Captain von Trapp uses an army whistle
to summon his children. My father

and stepmother own seven bird books.
Paperback, hardback. One signed

by Peterson, another inscribed
by my brother in '79: *Dear Mom,*

Merry Christmas! My stepmother,
at ninety-two, says: *Please take one.* My father,

also ninety-two, says: *Buy your own book!*
His way of saying he's not dead yet.

He doesn't know he has dementia.
We watch TV together. He loves

the commercials. In one, a turkey
drives a golf cart, relaxes at the beach,

reads a magazine. *Gone cold turkey,*
the voice says. And the turkey

does a dance, kicking its feet in the air.
A drug has curbed the turkey's cravings

for cigarettes. My father thinks the turkey
is real. *You can tell by the eyes,* he says.

During a commercial about Alzheimer's,
he doesn't say a word. The bird at the feeder

is real. We can tell by its hunger, its flight.
My father keeps eating his cereal.

My sister takes a picture of the bird,
clicking as quickly as she can, but the bird

is faster and the picture is a confusion
of wings, a blur which could be its own thing.

There's a story about God being bored:
when God's companions suggest a game

of hide-and-seek, they learn how good God is
at hiding. My father is different now.

Is he more himself? Or less? I like him this way.
I like the bird at the feeder, its confusion

of flight and hunger. I like the turkey
driving a golf cart, kicking its feet up.

My father was as afraid of his own father
as I was of mine. I want to believe in love,

I want to believe there is more love
somewhere.

The Life I Live

I could feel them looking up at me—
imaginary customers in a lightly furnished room—

as I scribbled orders on a small pad of paper.
I was nine, bringing make-believe food

to people in a hurry or on vacation. One, I remember,
was grieving. Another, I could tell, was in love.

Sometimes I imagine myself at ninety, somewhere north
forever cold, cradling a doll—my mind

as demented as my father's is now. The doll's eyes
opening and closing, making a soft clicking sound—

like an upturned beetle trying to right itself.
My daughter, neither born nor conceived,

splits my life in two directions. I like my life,
who I've become and who I love. Still, my mind

bears a creek deep enough for swimming,
children's shoes piling up by the back door.

My sorrow is as real as I am. Sometimes
I barely feel it—the way an animal, hibernating

in winter, might be cut and barely bleed.
Other times, the daughter I never had cups her hands

around fireflies—a glass jar on the grass beside her—
and asks *Why doesn't night stay in the jar?*

Joanna Macy says we must face our despair,
look right at it. Which is why I looked at George,

Hawaiian tree snail, last of his kind, dead
the first of the year. His death, symbolic

as it was real. When you give something a name,
people pay attention, and everyone said

he must have been lonely. Here's something
I can't name: the peace I felt while looking at his photo.

As if looking was a kind of love. Not enough,
but more than nothing at all. My daughter

is a lovely fiction. And god. What shall I do
with god? A priest held hostage for three years

celebrated communion every day with his fellow prisoners.
Body of Christ broken for you, as he distributed

the invisible bread. *Blood of Christ shed for you,*
pretending to lift a chalice of wine. Everyone said

what happened was real. My sorrow twists dolls
out of willow, buries them in the shade of an old tree.

My daughter presses her hands over my eyes.
Now you see me, now you don't. The doll's eyes

open and close. I'm happier than this poem says I am.
And also sadder. Maybe this will be enough: at ninety,

walking through snow, holding what isn't there
until what isn't there calls my name.

V

I Love

I love how my wife says *operators are standing by*,
whenever I'm out of town and she wants to chat.

I love that birds can see stars and that even fruit flies need sleep.

I love that an African grey parrot learned how to use 100 words
and that his last words were: *Be good* and *I love you*.

I love how Jesus stopped a crowd of men from stoning a woman just by
    writing in the sand.

I love that an octopus has three hearts.

I love that Mother Theresa only heard from God one time, and it was
    enough.

I love that some birds mate for life—and that after one dies,
the survivor sings both parts of their song.

I love that our brains are mostly water.

I love that some people believe in heaven. And some don't.

I love that an owl visited my wife in a dream and that my wife said hello and
    asked:
Are you the kind of owl that people refer to as a barred owl?

I love that what saves one person is not the same as what saves someone else.

I love how the word *cranium* sounds like the name of a flower.

I love that my mother keeps wanting to show me her garden.

I love that the owl answered back.

Notes

"Welcome": A couple of the stanzas in this poem (starting with *I never knew, on Tuesdays, what she'd look like*) were initially part of a much earlier poem that was published in my chapbook *Commemoration* (Finishing Line Press, 2012).

"Water Lessons": The image of a glass of water still sitting on a bureau of the Titanic and the phrase *strange physics* are from a science book I read in 2012 about the Titanic. I regret that I failed to adequately record the name and author of the book.

"Backstory": The italicized phrases are from the Nicene Creed (Lutheran Book of Worship).

"Underpinnings": The reference to a statue with a mouth that could be chanting or screaming was inspired from a passage in *Bog Bodies Uncovered: Solving Europe's Ancient Mystery* by Miranda Aldhouse-Green.

"Grief": The lines *like the black smoke of a squid, a fire / deep inside water* were inspired by a passage in Peter Godfrey-Smith's *Other Minds: The Octopus, the Sea, and the Deep Origins of Consciousness*.

"Meditations on My Mother's Death": The lines *Millions of unseen organisms die every second— / silent, bloodless* were inspired by a passage in E.O. Wilson's *Biophilia*. Also, two of the sections in this poem—the section that begins with *Inside the kitchen there was a boy* and the section that begins with *My grandfather*—were initially part of a much earlier poem that was published in my chapbook *Commemoration* (Finishing Line Press, 2012).

"Postcards from the 70s": In Section 1, the reference to *three houses down* is approximate.

"My Mother Is a Peaceful Ghost": The phrase *Divinity / diluted into nothingness* was inspired by the following response from theoretical physicist Lisa Randall (*Smithsonian Magazine*, 2013) about how the universe will end: "It will eventually radiate away and will eventually expand into dilute nothingness."

"Sheltering in Place": The niece in this poem is actually my great niece Amelia. Hi, Amelia!

"Love Poem for My Father": The phrase *This one's full of nuts* is from the cartoon contest in the July 2, 2018 issue of *The New Yorker*. The caption is from Jerry Chesterton of Wantagh, NY, and reads in full: "Most of them have candy. This one's filled with nuts."

"A white girl describes her neighborhood, 1980": *Imaginary waters / with real waters inside* is an allusion to the following line from Marianne Moore's poem "Poetry": *imaginary gardens with real toads in them.*

"Survival Guide for a Depressive": The Milky Way is called "backbone of night" by the people of South Africa who live in the Kalahari Desert and "winter street" by people in Sweden. *So many brains / all at once—in the sky* was inspired by a passage in Jennifer Ackerman's book *The Genius of Birds.*

"Broken Arm": The lines *and the future became the great homesickness. / Which is how some traditions refer to the divine* were inspired by Rainer Maria Rilke's description of God as the "great homesickness." The phrase *like salt dissolved in water* alludes to the way Brahman (ultimate reality) is described in certain traditions of Hinduism.

"New Bird": The phrase *there is more love somewhere* is from the African American hymn "There Is More Love Somewhere" as presented in the Unitarian Universalist hymnal *Singing the Living Tradition*.

"I Love": I learned about the African grey parrot (Alex) from Jennifer Ackerman's book *The Genius of Birds*.

Acknowledgments

Sincere gratitude to the editors of the following publications where these poems first appeared, at times in earlier versions:

All Things Jesbian: "Underpinnings"

Bellevue Literary Review: "Ars Poetica"

DMQ Review: "Grief" and "Survival Guide for a Depressive"

Great River Review: "Love Poem," "Interview," "The Life I Live," and "Backstory"

Narrative Magazine: "Broken Arm" and "Dementia Bus"

New Ohio Review: "Daughter Poem"

Ninth Letter: "Welcome"

RHINO Poetry: "The Last Time"

Rockhurst Review: "Water Lessohs"

Sinister Wisdom: "Meditations on My Mother's Death," "My Mother, Arriving," "My Mother Speaks to Me"

The Sun Magazine: "My Mother Is a Peaceful Ghost"

Continued thanks to Vanderbilt's MFA program, without which I probably wouldn't be doing any of this, especially to Kate Daniels, Rick Hilles, and Mark Jarman. Thanks also to the Vanderbilt Divinity School for its generous support during my MDiv program and for the myriad ways I was challenged and transformed—all for the better—during those years of study. Thank you especially to A.J. Levine, who helped me grow in ways I never thought possible.

Thank you to the following people for their writerly guidance, inspiration, and/or overall enthusiasm at various points along the way: Emily August, Elizabeth Barnett, Ellen Bass, Destiny Birdsong, Alicia Brandewie, Nickole Brown, Sheila Carter-Jones, Tiana Clark, Lee Conell, Sandy Spencer Coomer, Melissa Cundieff, Kendra DeColo, the late Claudia Emerson, Julie Enszer, Keegan Finberg, Stephanie Pruitt Gaines, Susan Gregg Gilmore, Jeff Hardin, Jessica Jacobs, Tanya Jarrett, Claire Jimenez, Donika Kelly, Sarah Kersh, Susanna Kwan, Amelia Martens, Linda Parsons, Molly Bess Rector, Nancy Reisman, Ciona Rouse, Freya Sachs, Jill Schepmann, Christina Stoddard, Meg Wade, Sarah Moore Wagner, David Winter, and Amy Wright.

Thank you to Louise LeBourgeois for her stunning artwork—and to Facebook for finally allowing our parallel Hyde Park lives to intersect!

Thank you to the following people for their love and support and overall awesomeness: Karyn, Dinah, Lorene, Staci, Marcy, Priscilla, Angie and Renee, Rachel and Andrea, Doug, Lizzie, Angela, Emily, Jamie, Kathi, Jenny, Nina, Rénee, Linda, Kerry, Ellin, George, Leah, David and Nickie.

Thank you to my family—my father and step-mother, my mother (who is ever-present), my siblings, nieces and nephews, cousins, and in-laws.

Thank you to Diane Goettel for giving both my first book *and* my second book such a wonderful home.

And to Laurie—again and always.

Photo: Beth Gwinn

Lisa Dordal holds a Master of Divinity and a Master of Fine Arts, both from Vanderbilt University, and teaches in the English Department at Vanderbilt. Her first full-length collection of poetry, *Mosaic of the Dark*, was a finalist for the 2019 Audre Lorde Award for Lesbian Poetry. She is a Pushcart Prize and Best-of-the-Net nominee and the recipient of an Academy of American Poets University Prize, the Robert Watson Poetry Prize from the Greensboro Review, and the Betty Gabehart Prize from the Kentucky Women Writers Conference. Her poetry has appeared in a variety of journals and anthologies including *Best New Poets, New Ohio Review, The Sun, Narrative, RHINO, Ninth Letter, CALYX, The Greensboro Review,* and *Vinyl Poetry.* Her website is lisadordal.com.